Q. What do the following have in common?

PIG SNOUT GLASSES

MUSIC TO MAIM BY

FAST-ITY BELT

PET HERPES

KITTY LITTER

A. Each of these items is fully described—along with everything from gross cosmetics to gross movies to gross vacations—in this thoroughly tasteless and tacky catalogue we call . . . **GROSS GIFTS!**

# GROSS GIFTS

By Julius Alvin

**ZEBRA BOOKS**
**KENSINGTON PUBLISHING CORP.**

ZEBRA BOOKS

are published by

KENSINGTON PUBLISHING CORP.

First printing: October, 1983

Printed in the United States of America

True to catalogue style, the author has included prices and suppliers in describing the items in this book. These descriptions are intended for **reading entertainment only,** and not as an endorsement.

# CONTENTS

# 1

# ART

## THE BLUE BOOK

THE BLUE BOOK is an all-color collection of sexual and humorous fantasies from more than 100 well known contemporary artists. Advertised as "All the Kink That's Fit to Ink." If you like paintings of a woman with a rose petal where her private parts should be, this is the book for you.

$18.95 plus $2.00 postage

Indigo Books
c/o American Showcase
724 Fifth Avenue
New York, NY 10019

## THE STANLEY GIRLS

Line drawings of "Beautiful, curvaceous Feminine" women—if you'd apply those adjectives to females who look like the Incredible Hulk. Set of five 8 x 10 drawings, $10.00.

DSG Products
P.O. Box 9694
Sacramento, CA 95823

## BIKER ART

Prints by Dave Mann painted exclusively for *Easyrider* Magazine. Only 300 printed of each—personally signed. $62.50 each.

Mackenzie Company
Box 29
Calabasas, CA 91302

## DONALD DUCK

Carl Barks, the artist who drew the Donald Duck and Uncle Scrooge comic books for 40 years, has done an oil painting of Donald, Scrooge and the kids in Scrooge's money bin. You can have a limited edition of the print of these famous fowl cartoon figures for the following prices:

Something New In

# GLAMOUR
## The Stanley Girls!

| | |
|---|---|
| First print | $1000.00 |
| 2-99 | $ 395.00 |
| 100-500 | $ 295.00 |

The Sharper Image
P.O. Box 26823
San Francisco, CA 94111

# 2

# BOOKS

*S-M: The Last Taboo* by Gerald and Caroline Greene (Grove Press, $2.95)

This book is described on the back cover as "the first book of sincerity." The authors consider S-M a "way of love based on the most intimate knowledge of the human soul." If you think pain is the way to rapture, this is the book for you.

*How to Pick Up Girls* by Eric Weber

According to the publisher, HOW TO PICK UP GIRLS has helped more men pick up more girls than any other book in the world . . . You'll learn: The best opening lines; How to get a girl horny; What makes a man sexy; Getting girls to pick you up.

If you need more advice after reading this

volume, you can order other books in the same line, such as HOW TO MAKE LOVE TO A SINGLE WOMAN and THE ART OF SENSUAL MESSAGE. Good luck.

HOW TO PICK UP GIRLS
$12.95 plus $2.00 shipping

Symphony Press
Box 515
Tenafly, NJ 07670

*Hiroshima and Nagasaki*

This massive (706 pages) paperback is a detailed study of what really happened in the two cities that were nuked in World War II. Very cheery reading in our nuclear world.

$15.95 plus $2.00 shipping

Clayton Survival Services
5026 Highway 140
Mariposa, CA 95338

*Up Yours: Guide to Advanced Revenge Techniques* by George Hayduke

The author of GET EVEN, Volumes 1 and 2, returns with "an outrageous compendium of wonderfully wicked ways to get even with the human vermin of this world." The catalogue copy always states it's sold "for entertainment purposes only." Sure.

$13.00 plus $2.00 Shipping

Ken Hale
P.O. Box 395
McDonald, OH 44437

*The Pearl* (Ballantine Books, $3.95)

*The Pearl* was an underground erotic journal first appearing in London in 1879 and published monthly until December, 1880. This book contains the entire contents of all eighteen issues, including six serialized novels ("Miss Pokingham, Or They All Do It;" "Miss Coote's Confession"). The book also contains hundreds of ribald poems, such as the following:

*When cunt first triumphed (as the learned suppose)*
*O'er failing pricks, Immortal Dildo rose,*
*From fucks unnumbered, still erect he drew*
*Exhausted cunts, and then demanded anew.*

*Bloody Iron: Practical Knife Fighting* by Harold Jenks & Michael Brown

The authors draw on their vast experience, learned both on the street and in federal prison. "They share secrets with you that could never have been learned elsewhere." Good.

$9.00 plus $2.00 shipping

Ken Hale
P.O. Box 395
McDonald, OH 44437

*Vampires Are* by Dr. Stephen Kaplan

Dr. Kaplan is the father of the infant science of vampirology. This is the first volume that argues the existence of living Draculas. He's preparing a second book based on the results of a scientific survey of 1000 people. Kaplan uncovered among that group 34 legitimate, human-blood-drinking vampires. He found the average male vampire was 5'10" tall, with brown hair and blue eyes, and 112 years old. Stay away from people with that description.

$9.95 hardcover        $4.95 paperback

ETC Publications
PO Drawer 1627A
Palm Springs, CA 92263

*Rude Food* by David Thorpe (Ballantine Books, $7.95)

This book is a collection of rather unusual combinations of food and naked bodies. An example: three oysters on the halfshell resting on a bed of seaweed placed over a woman's genital area. Bon appetit.

*The Wacky Humor of J. Kohl* (Hustler Magazine, $4.95)

One of the less crude cartoons in this volume shows an epilpetic with a dildo on his head, saying to his wife, "I feel another seizure coming on! Quick, Linda, sit on my head." The back cover bills Kohl as America's "most offensive cartoonist." That's truth in advertising.

*Death Log* by James Romenesko (Police Beat Press, $7.95)

The author says that this morbid manual detailing the deaths of such famous people as Marilyn Monroe, Natalie Wood, and Janis Joplin is being bought by "upper-class suburban housewives and business executives; people seeking a slice of life—or death—to which they've never been exposed." Yuch.

Available only by mail is the "first comprehensive listing of female fight sequences in the cinema." Ad-copy explains that "the confrontation between two (or more) women has been known and appreciated by film makers for years, because there is something special in these fights that, for want of a better description, touches the savage buried in all of us." Or some of us.

$20.00 plus $2.00 postage

Dugent Publishing Corporation
2355 Salzedo St.
Coral Gables, FL 33134

*Best Biker Fiction From Easyriders, No. 1 and 2*

No comment.

$3.00 each

Easyriders
P.O. Box 1025
Agoura, CA 91301

*Grande Illusions: The Art and Technique of Special Make-Up Effects* by Tom Savini (Starlog Press, $12.95)

The make-up genius behind the blood and gore in some of the most distasteful movies ever made (DAWN OF THE DEAD, MANIAC, FRIDAY THE 13TH) gives all the inside secrets of his gruesome art. Very useful in everyday life.

*The Nuclear War Fun Book* by Victor Langer and Walter Thomas (Owl Books, $5.95)

A book of fun things to do after civilization has been destroyed. Some examples: "Radio-active Tag—try to catch and contaminate others;" "Mark the Mutant;" "Nuclear Flash Shadow Pictures;" "Fun With Fallout." It's an anti-war satire—as much fun as THE CONCENTRATION CAMP COLORING BOOK.

*Extradition*

For $10.00, you get a list of foreign governments having extradition treaties with the U.S. The perfect gift for the international felons in your family. Send $10.00 to:

Information Unlimited
P.O. Box 21059
Sarasota, FL 33583

# 3

# CLOTHES

## BEER CAPS

Formal wear (perfect for weddings and funerals) in baseball caps adorned with the logos of 40 different brands of beer. Labels include: Budweiser, Natural Light, Michelob, Schlitz, Old Milwaukee, Blatz, Schmidt, Old Style, Colt 45, Lone Star, and Black Label. Price $7.99 plus $2.00 postage and handling.

AJD Cap Co.
3301 Castlewood Rd.
Richmond, VA

## NEW WAVE SHIRTS

Guaranteed to clash with everything you own. Comes in Blue and Red on white muscle shirt; Red and Black on white muscle shirt;

Black checks on white body, one Red, one Green sleeve.

$16.00 postpaid

The Alien Express Co.
51 East 42nd St.
New York, NY 10017

## SURGICAL SCRUB SUITS

Now, your favorite hospital wear is available in fashionable colors—purple, lavender, pink, turquoise, black, blue, white, green. $15.95 plus $2.00 shipping.

SOS Enterprises
Box 2026
Great Neck, NY 11022

## ALLERGY ON YOUR TIE

If you're into biology, you've got to have an anti-body cravat. The American Academy of Allergy and Immunology has designed a nifty necktie with an immunoglobulin molecule worked into the pattern. Sounds like nothing to sneeze at.

$20 Call (414) 272–6071

## SHOWING THE COLORS

Into nationalism? How about British flag, Rising Sun, American Flag, or Rebel flag shirts; or British flag shorts?

$13.50 postpaid

Robin Concepts
8033 Sunset Blvd., Suite 909
Hollywood, CA 90046

## RATS TO YOU

Tired of alligators on your shirt? Now you can get shirts and sweaters with a little rat on the breast—tres charming, eh?

Shirts $20.00                    Sweaters $24.00

Rat d'egout, Inc.
P.O. Box 40372
Cincinnati, Ohio 45240

## STAND OUT

"New padded brief [for men] 'lifts it up and points it out!' so you always look well endowed." $6.98

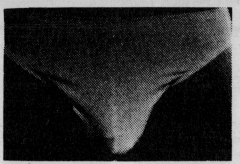

# STAND OUT!

**New padded brief "lifts it up and points it out" so you always look well endowed. Just $6.98.**

Adam and Eve
P.O. Box 900
Carrboro, NC 27510

## BODY ARMOR

It's a tough world out there, so many of us wouldn't be caught dead (so to speak) without body armor under our clothing—for work and play. Standard model (2 nine-layer armor panels and the standard carrier, $99.95) comes in Jungle Camo, Desert Camo, Undercover White, and Ninja Black. Extra protection available for more special occasions.

Silent Partner, Inc.
230 Lafayette St.
Gretna, LA 70053

## FETISH WEAR

Like to dress up like a studded snow tire? Then a place called Centurians is the mail order clothing house for you.

For information, contact: Centurians
P.O. Box AE
Westminster,
CA 92683

## FREDERICKS OF HOLLYWOOD

The most famous supplier of exotic lingerie and "daring sportswear." Some examples of lingerie:

1. Bare Sensation: Put your breasts on a shelf. Fiberfill shelves under each breast leave you free but supported. $13.50
2. The Venus Mini-Basque: "Be a naked goddess of love. Underwired, lace half-cups, black with turquoise beading, detachable garters and matching G-string. $28
3. The French Wench: Rosebuds and Pink ribbon trim for that "little girl" innocence. $28

# frederick's Classics

**Shape a BETTER Bottom. Frederick's PADDED Shapers Look so Real. He'll NEVER KNOW You Cheated!**

*Fix Your Flats*

...with Frederick's hip and fanny padder. Removable feather-weight pads **ROUND** out your hips, emphasize your derriere. **WIDE BAND** cinches the waist to show more hip curve. Satin control panel flattens the tummy. Removable garters. Nylon and spandex powernet. **NUDE.**
Waist sizes: Sm.( 22-25''), Med.( 26-27''), Lge.( 28-30''), or X-Lge.( 32-34'' ).

**#4-5424 $30**

Cinches Waist

Padded Fanny

Padded Hip

NOT a Girdle... a Padded Panty

REVERSIBLE Contour Pads. Wear HIGH (as shown) or REVERSE for a Natural Look

## Fanny Former ™

Cleavage so-o-o clever he'll never know you cheated. Soft, "silky" nylon panty. **PRE-SHAPED**, removable **PADS.** Center stretch seam for fanny shape and cleavage. **NUDE.**
Sm.( 22-25''), Med.( 26-27''), Lge.( 28-30''), or X-Lge.( 31-32'').

**#4-5315 2 for $27.88; $15 each**

4. Sugar 'N Spice: And everything naughty. Bare nipples are lifted by underwired, lace half-cups. Waist-nipper features, to contour boning to eliminate midriff bulge. Opens in back. $18.50

5. French Secret: Underwired waist-slimmers nips and lifts to transform your body into a lovely hourglass silhouette. Rose patterned black with red satin ribbon trim. $30

6. Fanny Former: Panties with feather weight removable hip and fanny pads to give a more rounded shape.

7. Real Silk Crotchless Panties: The ultimate thrill . . . 100% silk, tiny bow trim. In Black, Beige, or Red. $7.50

8. Silk G-strings: "Keep it brief and sex-citing. Barely covers your assets." 3 for $15

9. Tiger-print Cat Suit: "Sizzling tiger stripes stretch taut over every delectable curve." $29

10. Baby Doll & Bikini Set: "Sexy satin buccaneer collar and cuffs set off a totally sheer nylon shirt. Matching satin G-String." $20

11. Fishnet Body Suit: "An x-rated feature he'll want to see again and again! Naughty body-baring fishnet." $39.

12. Naughty Crotchless Victorian Pajama: "See-through. Sizzling Red bows for

him to untie, convenient front hook." $32

13. Shocking Stocking: Stays up without garter belt. $6
14. Grecian Glamour: "Entice him in this sensuous toga-style baby doll. Pink embroidery trims waist-plunging neckline. Daring halter reveals your provocatively bare backside." $20
15. Instant Love: "Satin sleepshirt slips on and off in an instant. Reveals you through side slits and lush dyed-to-match lace." $18

For information and catalog:

Fredericks of Hollywood
P.O. Box 4531
Los Angeles, CA 90051

## JAPANESE UNDERWARE

Looking for oriental delights? For $55 you get:
Japanese Nite Gown (nemaki) for man and woman
Instant Cock Cover (fundoshi)
Pink Rose Protect (koshimaki)
Send money order to: Friendship Society
113 Box, Ito-pia,
1-6-1, Kaigan
Minato-ku, Tokio
JAPAN

# TOO GROSS TO TITLE

Men's briefs imprinted "I Gotta Whopper"
$4.00

Adolf's
2607 Hennepin
Minneapolis, MN 55408

Candy Pants: Edible, cherry flavored
women's briefs

$5.50

Stamford Hygienic
P.O. Box 932
Stamford, CT 06904

# NASTY LEATHER

The finest in biker wear:

1. Bitchin' Britches: Leather pants with custom-design boot cut. $180
2. Bar Hopper: Nasty leather racing jacket. $175
3. Ultimate Chaps: Top grade American leather wraps all the way around your legs . . . Full length flaps cover the zippers, protecting you from the wind and your bike from zipper scratches. $160.

4. For Denim Diggers: Classic jean jacket designed in cowhide. $160

Easyriders
Box 1025
Agora, CA 91301

## MACHO HEADWEAR

Special Forces Green Beret. Pretend you were a rough, tough "Green Beanie" at the Nam. $13.75

Kaufman's West
504 Yale SE
Albuquerque, NM 87106

## U.S. ARMY BATTLEDRESS

Complete outfitting for your next war in any terrain. Styles include:
1. U.S. Marine Corp Recon Tiger Stripes
2. O.D. Green
3. S.W.A.T. Black
4. Day Desert
5. Night Desert (Special Anti-Starlight Scope Treated)
6. Woodland
7. U.S. Marine Corps Camouflage (Jungle Fatigues)

Jackets $29.95                    Trousers $29.95

Also complete line of jackets, hats,
boots, etc.

Parellex Corporation
1285 Mark St.
Bensenville, IL 60106

## UP AND COMING

A line of very brief underpants for men.
Some examples:

1. The Net: "Will catch her by surprise
   when she says that only the sheerest
   mesh stands between you and her."
   $4.95
2. Handsome Handful: Female hand
   painted onto crotch of briefs. $6.50
3. Lance Alot: "Sheer, see-through bikini
   barely keeps your swords sheathed until
   you ride to rescue her." $6.95
4. Solid Gold: Will turn your woman into
   a "gold digger." $6.95
5. Moonshine: "This see-thru, open in
   back brief in bad-guy black is so
   arousing it should be illegal." $6.50
6. The Predator: "This leopard print nylon
   tricot bikini keeps you tightly poised
   until you're ready to trot." $6.95

7. Oh Captain, My Captain: "Sheerest nylon front and airy fishnet back." $5.50

8. Swashbuckler: A posing strap with interlocking buckles: $6.95

9. Disco Fever: Lavender nylon with wild black fringe. $6.95

10. Jewel Thief: "Before you steal her crown jewels, hide your pride and joy in the sheerest pouch with rhinestones." $6.95

Stamford Hygienic
P.O. Box 932
Stamford, CT. 06904

# 4

# COSMETICS

*POTENT-8*

"Start a spontaneous reaction in anyone you desire! . . . Potent-8 contains pheromones— powerful sexual attractants whose scent can be used to arouse any woman and release her inhibitions." $9.95 plus $1.50 postage and handling

BodyScience
P.O. Box 1045
Scarsdale, NY 10583

BODY GLITTER

"Apply body glitter on all the important areas to add a sensuous sparkle—especially in the dark—so your lover can hit all the right targets. Also a festive touch for a shimmery face." Comes in silvery Opalescent and glowing Rainbow Sunset.

$6.00 plus $1.00 postage

Pleasure Products
P.O. Box 5973–198
Sherman Oaks,
CA 91413

## ANDROS

"It really makes women want you . . . [we have] managed to isolate and concentrate the smell of male sex appeal—Androsten—and combine it with a musky, male-scented cologne and aftershave. ABSOLUTELY FULLY GUARANTEED." $9.95 plus $1.95 postage

Kent Institute, Inc.
P.O. Box 214
Mt. Morris, IL 61054

## THE BLOOD BOUTIQUE

Want to give your lover or boss a little zinger? Tired of being pushed around on the beach or in the subway? This stuff's for you:

1. Derma Wax (mortician's wax): Distort

yourself with bumps, scars, warts, etc.) 1.75 oz., $3.25

2. Nose Putty $3.25 per stick
3. Liquid Latex: Dries to solid rubber, used for making bald caps, reusable scars, etc. 1 oz. $3.25
4. Makeup Pencils: Come in Gash Red, Vein Blue, Jaundiced Yellow, Silverized Green, Silverized Violet. $1.25
5. ZAUDER's Crepe Hair: Unravels to produce mounds of wild, unruly hair. Comes in 13 colors from White to Bright Green. $1.75.
6. Rigid Collodion: "When brushed on skin, dries to a scarred appearance. 1 oz, $2.75
7. Blood for formal wear: ". . . has the sheen, consistency, and color of the real thing." 1.5 oz., $5.75
8. Blood capsules: "Bite into 'em—they mix with saliva to produce plenty of you-know-what. They taste good, too!" 10-$3.50

Send $2.00 postage with order to:

FANGORIA
Starlog Press
475 Park Ave. South
New York, NY 10016

# 5

# CRAFTS

## CLEAN AND DIRTY DISHWASHER MAGNETS

These soft-sculpture magnet kits, which comes with "pre-made head, material, felt, yarn, beads, sewing kit, and pattern," make a perfect gift for those unfortunates who can't figure out whether the dishes in the washer are clean or dirty.

$4.99 plus $2.00 postage

See-Me Dolls
P.O. Box 3004
Simi Valley, CA 93063

## ADOPTION PAPERS FOR DOLLS

"Beautifully styled pair includes our unique

Certificate of Animated Birth. Satisfaction guaranteed." $4.00

Lavender House
Box 17679
Nashville, TN 37217

## DOORSTOP PATTERNS

Slam Mr. and Mrs. Santa Claus with your bedroom door. If you don't like your presents, you can even kick Saint Nick around. Kits $3.75 for both.

Hollow Tree Crafts
29680 Edwards
Livonia, MI 48154

## NO HALF-BAKED IDEA

"Turn flour/salt/water into terrific projects" —and make a fine mess of your kitchen at the same time. And what could be a better Christmas present than dough?

Two Books: *You Can Dough It*
*Let's Dough It Again*

Hot Off The Press
7212 S. Seven Oaks, Dept. 31
Canby, Oregon 97013

# 6

# DRUGS

"THE SPURIOUS LINE":

Spurious Spanish Fly Drops $4.95
Spurious Nymphomaniac Drops $4.95
Spurious Hard-on Drops $4.95
Spurious Knock-out Pills $5.95
Spurious Hypnotic Pills $5.95
Spurious Spanish Fly Sugar $4.95

All available from Valentine Products, Inc., P.O. Box 6400, Newtown, CT 06470. Add $1.95 for each product for postage and handling.

"LOVE DROPS"

"LOVE DROPS are a must for the man who has difficulty getting women to cooperate. Just two drops will turn-em-on and put them sex-

two drops will turn-em-on and put them sexually in your power. Works on young girls or older women."

Sold by POW Products, 7313 Melrose Ave., Los Angeles, CA 90046. $6 for 30 day supply.

## "NON-PRESCRIPTION STIMULANTS"

Magazines are filled with ads for "stimulants" and "diet aids" that are packaged as look-alikes for prescription drugs like dexedrine. These tablets generally contain large doses of caffeine with other substances like ephendrine sulphate, phenylpropanolamine, or benzocaine. E.G.:

"Amphetrazine—Continuous Action Stimulants"

Capsules: Small Black
Large Black
Small Yellow
Large Yellow
Blue/Clear
Green/Clear

"Stimulants are F.D.A. categorized as decongestants and labeled as such. CAUTION: Pregnant women, persons over 65 and individuals with high blood pressure, heart disease, diabetes or thyroid disease should use only as directed by a physician. Products not intended for repackaging or resale. Individuals involved in resale should register with proper authorities and/or consult an attorney."

Jars of 100 tablets, $19.95 plus handling

Brant Pharmacal
(419) 698-9974

## INCENSE—THE NATION'S HOTTEST PRODUCT

"Superior-Caine" (Snow White) 2gm. $12.00
"Super Toot"                    1.5gm. $10.00
"Pseudo-Caine (Crystalized)  1.5gm. $10.00

Main Labs
(313) 847-0617

## YOHIMBE

"As seen on national television and reported in the August 1982 issue of Science Digest, Doctors Alvaro Morales, urologist, and David Surridge, psychiatrist, both of Queen's University in Ontario discovered during testing that men with organic impotency responded to the African aphrodisiac Yoimbine, a derivative of yohimbe tree bark.

"While taking yohimbe, 60% REGAINED FULL HARD ERECTIONS, ORGASM AND EJACULATION."

1/4 Oz. (3 week supply) $6.95 + $2 postage

Yohimbe
1626 North Wilcox
Hollywood, CA 90028


## PECKER UPPERS

"Can't stay hard? Ejaculate prematurely? PECKER UPPERS are the answer to your problem. One potent capsule will rejuvenate your sex drive, make you rock hard and delay your climax as long as you want. Make her cum, cum and cum!"

30 day supply $6.00

Park Medical Lab
7313 Melrose Ave.
Los Angeles, CA 90046


## FOOD FOR THOUGHT

"As one grows older . . . it is believed that memory power decreases. Not necessarily so! At any age . . . memory efficiency can be improved if we make sure to nourish the brain with the nutrients that are known to stimulate maximum mental performance. MEMO-REX contains the nutrients that can pass through the blood-brain barrier and help feed the brain hemispheres! A Nourished Brain Helps You Into New Thinking Directions!"

50 tablets          $4.95

STUR-DEE Health Products, Inc.
Island Park, NY 11558

NSP-270

"NOW! A GUARANTEED 'SEX PILL' FOR MEN!" reads the ad. Sub headlines include: "U.S. Navy Uses This Discovery to Give Men Dramatic Increases in Penis Size." The benefits include "amazing spurts of penis growth" and "sensational ejaculations."

One bottle of regular strength NSP-270 $6.95 plus $.90 postage from Frank E. Bush, Inc., 535 5th Avenue, New York, NY 10017.

SUN TAN PILLS

"VITA-TAN tablets contain our exclusive 3-way formula used by millions of Europeans for an absolutely safe, positively stunning TAN WITHOUT THE SUN. Now, regardless of skin type, you can have the tan you always wanted in as little as two weeks."

80 tablets          $19.95

C.J. Sales
Box 30554
Seattle, WA 98103

# 7

# EDUCATIONAL ASSISTANCE

## COLLEGE DIPLOMA—ONE DAY

"DIPLOMA LOST, DAMAGED, ETC. Exacting reproduction; immediate, confidential service. Color catalog/School list $3.00"

Alumni Arts
Box 552
Grants Pass, OR 97526

## THESIS FOR HIRE

College Students! Improve your grades! Research catalog — 356 pages, 10,278 topics. $1.00

Research
Box 25916G
Los Angeles, CA 90025

## UNIVERSITY DEGREES BY MAIL

For $35, Dr. John Bear will provide College Degree Counseling. Also included, not incidentally, is a list of names, addresses, and details of "virtually every diploma mill operating in the U.S., Canada, and Europe." Be a Ph.D. without leaving your living room.

Dr. John Bear
P.O. Box 11447-E7
Marina Del Rey, CA 90291

## RELIGIOUS INSTRUCTION

For those students called to the cloth who can't stand the thought of years of study, try the following:

1. "Become an ordained minister. Free ministerial credentials legalize your right to the title 'Reverend'."

Church of Gospel Ministry
486-NE Skyhill Court
Chula Vista, CA 92010

2. "Become Legally ordained minister. Credentials sent for $3.00."

American Fellowship Church
469 E. Pacific
Monterey, CA 93942

3. "Become ordained Baptist minister immediately."

Seminary
Box 322
Indianola, Iowa 50125

# 8

# GAMES

## FOR LOVERS ONLY

"Adult candle-lit games you can play with your lover. Reach the climax together." $8.95

Stamford Hygienic
P.O. Box 932
Stamford, CT 06904

## DIRTY WORDS

"Deluxe Dirty Words . . . combine otherwise ordinary words into implicative sentences." E.G., "Lick my pink banana"; "My bare mango is hot"; "Is he a good pump?" $14.00 plus $3.00 postage

PARAMAIL
P.O. Box 15457
Salt Lake City, Utah 84115

## TAKE IT OFF

Party games for those who like to "take it all off":
SCREW UP
SIP & GO NAKED
HOP SCOTCH
SPIN THE BOTTLE
TIC-TAC STRIP
PAIR UP—PEEL OFF
SIP & STRIP

Adolf's
2607 Hennepin
Minneapolis, MN 55408

## VICE DICE

"The X-rated adult game that will have everyone rollin' around in wild sex action with every roll of the dice. Certain to turn any party into an orgy of lusty fun." $9.95

Pleasure Products
P.O. Box 5973-198
Sherman Oaks, CA 91413

# NAUGHTY CARDS

"52 sexy adults-only playing cards. Features couples in X-rated sex positions." $6.50

Stamford Hygienic
P.O. Box 932
Stamford, Ct. 06904

"Nude men playing cards . . . there's a different joker on every card." $4.50

Adolf's
2607 Hennepin
Minneapolis, MN 55408

# 9

# GREETING CARDS

## NICE 'N' SLEAZY

This outfit has such cards as:
1. "Buns For Your Birthday"—a picture of buttocks in a gift box.
2. "Happy Birthday you little prick" A monkey with a very red erection.
3. "Happy Birthday, you asshole!" A monkey with his rear opening showing.

Nice 'n' Sleazy
1560 Broadway, Suite 807
New York, NY 10036

## T.N.T. DESIGNS

1. "Love Comes In Spurts" A young woman massaging breast which is issuing a torrent of milk.

2. "So You Think You've Got Everything" A very erotic figure with a beautiful face, well developed breasts—and a rather large penis.

T.N.T. Designs
35 W. 24th St.
New York, NY 10010

## ROCKSHOTS

1. "Yes, Vagina, There Is A Santa Claus" Saint Nick peering under the dress of a young girl.
2. "Born to Get Old" a group of elderly people in biker outfits.

Rockshots
51 W. 21st. St.
New York, NY 10010

# 10

# JOB OPPORTUNITIES

## REAL ESTATE FORECLOSURE

"Horizon Financial Corporation is a Florida corporation that deals with locating and acquiring distressed real estate. The course that is presented to you will show how to locate these properties, evaluate them and be able to purchase them below market value without cash or a minimum capital outlay."

Home Study Course in this lovely field: $55.00

Horizon Financial Corporation
2474 N. Federal Highway
Pompano Beach, Florida 33064

## BOUNTY HUNTING

"Legal for anyone and very profitable! For

legal statutes and employment information, send $2.00 and SASE."

Research Unlimited
Box 152
Depew, NY 14043

# ADVENTURING

"Income opportunities for adventurers. Free information with SASE."

Adventurers
P.O. Box 1160
Pacifica, CA 94044

# RIDING SHOTGUN

"Travel aboard yachts to Hawaii, Caribbean, Bahamas. Scott Barrie and Associates is taking applications from persons experienced in the use of modern weapons to 'ride shotgun' for the owners of these boats."

Send $1.00 to: Scott Barrie and Assoc.
P.O. Box 87
Brandenton Beach, FL 33510

## PROCESS SERVER

"Earn $12.00 to $20.00 per unit. Business booming. Free information-decal."

Process Server
Box 314-F
Boston, MA 02188

## MECHANICAL BIRD SALES

"If you qualify, our program will show you how to set up two or three part-time teenagers (on commission), who could earn you up to $1,000.00 per weekend."

"Our newest, ultra-hot product, you wind up and—flapping its wings like crazy—it looks like a real bird, and flies hundreds of feet with no lead wires or strings."

3 birds plus manual        $19.95

J & R Sunshine and Cheer Office
4919 - 48 St.
Red Deer, Alberta
CANADA T4N 1S8

## MAILING LIST PROTECTION AGENT

"You, as a Mailing List Protection Agent, will have your address and a code name used as a decoy . . . This is an on-going endeavor that you can participate in for as long as you like, and really earn up to $275.00 per week."

"In order to get officially registered as a Mailing List Protection Agent, you must pay a one time fee as indicated on the LIFETIME REGISTRATION CERTIFICATE."

Send $25.00

U.S. List Protection Company
Suite 760, Keystone Executive Plaza
12555 Biscayne Blvd.
Miami, FL 33181

# 11

# JOKE BOOKS

*GROSS JOKES* by Julius Alvin

The biggest, funniest, and grossest of the gross joke books. The dedication of this offensive but hilarious volume reads: "In fond memory of Helen Keller." Sample jokes:

Why does Helen Keller masturbate with one hand?
So she can moan with the other.

Why do farts smell?
So deaf people can enjoy them, too.

$2.50 plus $.50 for postage and handling

Zebra Books
475 Park Avenue South
New York, NY 10016

## TOTALLY GROSS JOKES by Julius Alvin

More disgusting hilarity by the master of perversity, Julius. A sample:

What do you call a black with no arms?
Honest.

$2.50 plus $.50 for postage and handling

Zebra Books
475 Park Avenue South
New York, NY 10016

## TRULY TASTELESS JOKES by Blanche Knott (Ballantine Books, $2.25)

A funny and decidedly tasteless collection of the worst kind of humor. An example:

Why does Helen Keller wear skin tight pants?
So that people can read her lips.

## TRULY TASTELESS JOKES TWO by Blanche Knott (Ballantine Books, $2.25)

A sequel to the above. A sample:

Why do Italian men have moustaches?
So they can look like their mothers.

*THE WORLD'S BEST DIRTY JOKES and MORE OF THE WORLD'S BEST DIRTY JOKES* by Mr. "J" (Ballantine Books, $2.25 each)

Two collections of longer jokes, most of which have been around for quite a few years. An example:

The young farmer's helper was telling his friend about his wedding night.

"Boy, is my wife dumb!" he exclaimed. "We got into bed, and she put her pillow under her ass instead of her head."


*THE OFFICIAL DIRTY JOKE BOOK* by Larry Wilde (Pinnacle Books, $2.25)

A thick collection with the hilarious kernels buried among a lot of chaff. An example:

Bill: I think I'm starting to walk in my sleep.
Will: What makes you think that?
Bill: I woke up in my own bed this morning.

# 12

# JEWELRY

## X-RATED WATCH

Just what you've always wanted. Not only does this Quartz LCD Chronograph/Chronometer tell you the time and date, act as a stopwatch, and serve as an alarm, but it provides an X-rated movie with musical accompaniment. We see a boy meet girl, they both do a strip tease, the girl kneels for oral sex, then they make love. Watch is advertised as an exciting way to "MEET NEW GIRLS . . . IMPRESS FRIENDS . . . BE THE LIFE OF THE PARTY." Sure.

$39.95 plus $2.50 postage

21st Century Products
2105 Lakeland Ave.
Ronkonkoma, NY 11779

## RINGS AND EARRINGS

If you're stuck for a birthday or Christmas present for the one you love, there's something for everyone in the following list:

### Rings (Sterling Silver)

| | | | |
|---|---|---|---|
| Devil | $40 | Succubus | $40 |
| Devilbat | $50 | Swastika | $45 |
| Dragon | $45 | Tiger | $30 |
| Hatchetface | $60 | Christ | $45 |
| Horned cyclops | $60 | Cyclops | $40 |
| Reaper | $60 | Eye | $25 |

Mac

Hatchetface

Devilbat

Horned cyclops

Fool

30 m.m.

| Serpent | $40 | Frog | $20 |
|---|---|---|---|
| Warlord | $50 | Lips | $20 |
| Deathchief | $40 | Nazi-eagle | $45 |
| Deathdealer | $75 | Ram | $40 |
| Jesus | $45 | Satyr | $40 |
| Lobo | $40 | Skull | $40 |
| Madmax | $60 | Spaceface | $40 |
| Nazi Wed. Bd. | $30 | Tinyskull | $15 |
| Nightmare | $50 | Vampire bitch | $40 |
| Nude | $45 | Viking | $40 |
| Pirate | $75 | Wall | $45 |
| S.S. Skull | $40 | | |

## Earrings (Sterling Silver—$20 a pair)

| | |
|---|---|
| Arch-demon | Nazi-eagle |
| Ax | Nightflyer |
| Bat | Reaper |
| Bat II | Rodent |
| Bird | Satyr |
| Blade | Skeleton |
| Cybot | Swastika |
| Fairy | Unicorn |
| Freedom | Wolf |
| Half-skull | |
| Leaf | |
| Lightning | |

## LEATHER GOODS

Something to wear for any formal occasion, like busting up a new tavern:

Belts

| | |
|---|---|
| Spike Belt | $21 |
| Square Stud Belt | $24 |
| Wings-jeweled | $21 |
| Harley wings | $16 |

## WRIST BANDS

Studded wrist bands from $4 to $19. Studded watchbands from $9 to $14.

Adolf's
2607 Hennepin
Minneapolis, MN 55408

## CHAIN BRACELET

Real bike chains in gold or silver. $3.95

Adolf's
2607 Hennepin
Minneapolis, MN 55408

## NECKLACES

1. Horses' Ass Neck: "Make a presentation to one! Unisex." $5.00
2. Dirty Monkey: "Monkey has 'it' right in his hand." $3.95

3. "I feel" Necklace: "Just give it a turn to 'hot,' 'shitty,' 'horny,' etc." $5.95

Adolf's
2607 Hennepin
Minneapolis, MN 55408

# 13

# MEDICAL AIDS

HEIGHT INCREASE

" 'You can add 2-4 inches in 10 weeks or less,' says William A Reldnas.

'I have positive proof you can increase your height. Here are the indisputable facts. For many years, scientists believed height increase was not possible after the end of childhood. Recent factual data proves they were wrong.' "

THE HEIGHT INCREASE METHOD
$19.95 plus $1.00 postage

The Height Report, Inc.
2105 Lakeland Ave.
Ronkonkoma, NY 11779

# Are You Too Short?

## "You can add 2-4 inches in 10 weeks or less!"
### Says William A. Reldnas

"I have positive proof you can increase your height. Here are the indisputable facts.

"For many years, scientists believed height increase was not possible after the end of childhood. Recent factual data proves they were wrong. If athletes can increase the length of their limbs AFTER the age of puberty, you can certainly increase the length of your legs and complete torso and, you can do it scientifically, without artificial contraptions or possible injury by using The Height Increase Method."

While it may not yet be acceptable scientific dogma, the research sources are well known and respected scientific journals. And what's more important, if you're not 100% satisfied that *The Height Increase Method* is living up to all of Reldnas's claims, simply send it back for an immediate refund, no questions asked. Isn't that fair? Order your copy right away. Do it now!

© 1982 The Height Report, Inc.

# THE BREAST LOVER

"A pleasurable, satisfying way to enlarge your breasts. Tugs at your nipples and applies suction to enlarge your breasts." $17.95

Stamford Hygienic
P.O. Box 932
Stamford, CT 06904

# 14

# MILITARY MEMORABILIA

## NAZI MEMENTOS

Nothing like impressing your friends and neighbors with a Nazi "Concentration Camp Inspectorate Staff collar tab, sleeve badge, and sleeveband." Parade around the backyard in your S.S. service tunics and caps. Adorn your clothing with Nazi "skull-crossbones" metal and cloth emblems. Stun your date by arriving in a Waffen SS Wolfshead smock: For accenting your formal wear, how about a "Race and Rehabilitation Office" sleeve diamond?

Complete catalog of these and other militaria from:

Krupper Militaria
Box 177, Salina Station
Syracuse, NY 13208

## NAZI DISPLAYS

| | |
|---|---|
| Nazi Burial Flag | $39.00 |
| Nazi Armband | $ 7.00 |
| German Helmets (Steel) | $ 29.00 |
| Helmet Decals (SS, Swastika, Iron Cross) | $ .50 for 2 |
| Tie Tacks | $ 3.00 for 2 |
| Iron-On Transfers | $ 2.00 |

Africa Corps
Luftwaffe
Swastika
Maltese Cross
SS
Army
Death Head
Police

Adolf's
2607 Hennepin
Minneapolis, MN 55408

## U.S. MEDALS AND CERTIFICATES

You can be a hero, right in your own living room. Display the following:

**Medals**

| | |
|---|---|
| Medal of Honor | Price upon request |
| Distinguished Service Cross | $125.00 |

# R.u.S.-Hauptamt

ALLGEMEINE-SS
Race & Rehab
Head Office sleeve
badge & sleeveband

SS-TV
Concentration Camp Inspectorate Staff collar tab,
sleeve badge & sleeveband

SS-TV
Training Camp
Dachau Staff
collar tab

# SS-Totenkopfverbände

| | |
|---|---|
| Navy Cross | $150.00 |
| Distinguished Service Medal | |
|    Army | $150.00 |
|    Navy-Marine Corps | $150.00 |
|    Air Force | $125.00 |
|    Coast Guard | $150.00 |
| Silver Star | $ 40.00 |
| Purple Heart | $ 40.00 |
| Viet Nam Service Medal | $ 15.00 |

## Certificates

| | |
|---|---|
| Medal of Honor | $550.00 |
| Distinguished Service Cross | $250.00 |
| Distinguished Service Medal | $250.00 |
| Silver Star | $150.00 |
| Bronze Star | $150.00 |
| Purple Heart | $150.00 |
| Honorable Discharge | $500.00 |
| Dishonorable Discharge | $ 50.00 |

Martin Lederman
21 Naples Road
Brookline, Massachusetts 02146

## I.D. CARDS AND CERTIFICATES

"C.I.A., Special Forces, Rangers, Seal Team, Recon, Scout-Sniper, S.O.G., Para-Rescue, Airborne, Weapons Expert . . . With your name, rank, units, etc."

Illustrated brochure     $1.00

Kenwood Associates
Box 66
Long Green, MD 21092

## BATTLE FLAGS

Viet Cong, North Vietnamese Army, and Commie battle flags. "Excellent wall displays."

$15.00 each

Martial Sales
Box 71395
New Orleans, LA 70172

# 15

# MOVIES

*Pink Flamingos* 1972, Directed by John Waters

Although he'd produced previous epics like
MONDO TRASHO and MULTIPLE
MANIACS, it was PINK FLAMINGOS that
established John Water's reputation as "the
prince of puke." The culmination of this
exercise in perversion is when the star, 300
pound transvestite Divine, sees a small dog
shitting. He/she rambles over, picks up the
excrement, and eats it. Yes, fans, it's no special
effect—Divine really ate dog turds. Yuch.

*Salo, the 120 Days of Sodom* 1977, Directed by
Pier Paolo Pasolini

This pseudo-art film is a two hour exercise
in sadism and torture. A group of Fascists
kidnap teenagers, and abuse them in every

graphic, obscene way from eye-gouging to dismemberment. In the film's main banquet, all the food is human excrement. This film was banned in Italy, which shows you how gross it truly is.

*Texas Chainsaw Massacre* 1974, Directed by Tobe Hooper

Don't eat for a couple days before you view this 87 minute exercise in butchery, which was based on the story of Wisconsin murderer Ed Gein, who dug up dead bodies for food and wore human skin. Five unfortunates, including a cripple, fall prey to "Leatherface", a charming hulk in a mask made of human skin, who runs around dismembering folks with a gleaming chainsaw. After watching all the flesh and blood in this awesomely gruesome epic, you'll be a vegetarian for weeks.

*The Exorcist* 1973, Directed by William Friedkin

Why did poor Linda Blair have to wallow in green vomit and masturbate with a cross? Even worse, the huge box office success of this film resulted in THE EXORCIST II, a triumph of illogical idiocy starring Richard Burton and an overstuffed Linda Blair. Give us a break.

*Dawn of the Dead* 1978, Directed by George Romero

This movie is a sequel to the famous NIGHT OF THE LIVING DEAD, in which a group of zombies gnawed on human flesh while they stalked a group of young people trapped in an abandoned house. In DAWN OF THE DEAD, the zombies are outnumbering the people, and, if you pardon the expression, all hell breaks loose. What makes DAWN more gut-wrenchingly gross than NIGHT is that the second film is in color. By the time you see the zombies munching on intestines, you'll be heading for the rest room.


*Basket Case* 1982, Directed by Frank Henen-lotter

Hands down winner of the "gross concept" award. A teenager arrives at a run-down New York City hotel carrying a large wicker basket, into which he periodically shoves hamburgers and other goodies. We soon learn that the teenager was born with the mutated remains of a Siamese twin attached to his chest. The hunk of flesh, named Belial, is still alive—claws, sharp fangs, and all.

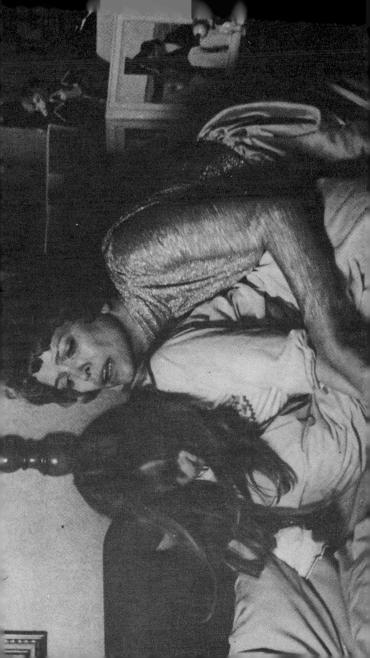

# An AVALANCHE of KILLER WORMS
## ...writhing across the land in a tidal wave of terror!

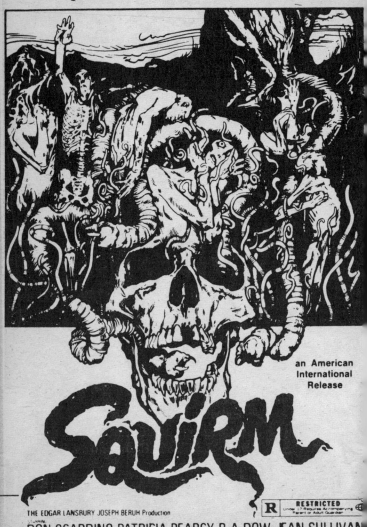

an American
International
Release

*Squirm*

THE EDGAR LANSBURY JOSEPH BERUH Production

STARRING
DON SCARDINO PATRICIA PEARCY R.A. DOW JEAN SULLIVAN

EXECUTIVE
PRODUCERS EDGAR LANSBURY & JOSEPH BERUH PRODUCER GEORGE MANASSE

MUSIC COMPOSED BY ROBERT PRINCE WRITTEN AND DIRECTED BY JEFF LIEBERMAN COLOR BY MOVIEL

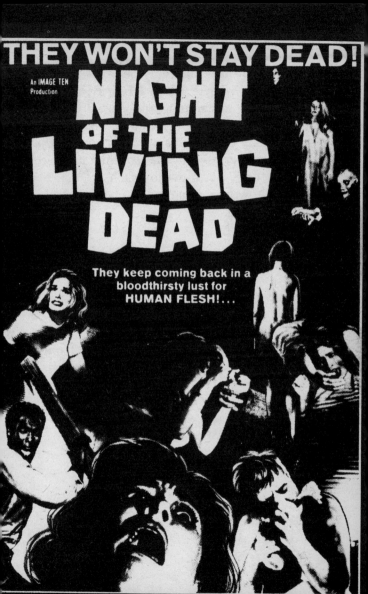

THEY WON'T STAY DEAD!

An IMAGE TEN Production

# NIGHT OF THE LIVING DEAD

They keep coming back in a bloodthirsty lust for HUMAN FLESH!...

"Those who go beneath the surface do so at their own peril."
Oscar Wilde

*Snuff* 1976, Credits not released

"The film that could only be made in South America . . . where life is CHEAP" read the posters. The ad campaign purported that this was a true "snuff" film—that the female star was actually killed on camera. Of course, that was a pile of crap—but the fact that audiences could actually be drawn by such a claim is a proof of how base some human beings can be. The pits!

## Gross Movie Titles

*Attack of the Killer Tomatoes*
*Blood Orgy of the She Devils*
*Breakfast at Manchester Morgue*
*Children Shouldn't Play with Dead Things*
*Doctor Butcher, Medical Deviate*
*Eaten Alive*
*The Gore Gore Girls*
*Hag in a Black Leather Jacket*
*I Dismember Mama*
*Ilsa, She-Wolf of the SS*
*Jesse James Meets Frankenstein's Daughter*
*Nazi Love Camp*
*One Thousand Convicts and One Woman*
*Please Don't Eat My Mother*
*The Rats Are Coming, The Werewolves
  Are Here*
*Shriek of the Mutilated*
*Teenage Psycho Meets Bloody Mary*

YOU'RE INVITED
TO ORVILLE'S "COMING-OUT" PARTY...
It'll Be A Scream... YOURS!

P.S.

# CHILDREN SHOULDN'T
# PLAY WITH
# DEAD THINGS!

A BENJAMIN CLARK FILM
STARRING  ALAN ORMSBY · JANE DALY · ANYA ORMSBY · JEFFREY GILLEN
VALERIE MAMCHES · PAUL CRONIN and SETH SKLAREY AS ORVILLE

MUSIC BY CARL ZITTRER · PRODUCED BY BENJAMIN CLARK & GARY GOCH
WRITTEN & DIRECTED BY  BENJAMIN CLARK
RELEASED THRU GENENI FILM DISTRIBUTING CO. COLOR.

PG
PARENTAL GUIDAN

# 16

## KIDS' TOYS

*THE MARILYN MONROE COLLECTION*

Commemorate her suicide and give your daughter the doll of a woman who's a wonderful role model for American womanhood. These lifelike representations show Marilyn in costumes from HOW TO MARRY A MILLIONAIRE, GENTLEMEN PREFER BLONDES, THERE'S NO BUSINESS LIKE SHOW BUSINESS, and THE SEVEN YEAR ITCH.

16" dolls $49.95
11-½" dolls $24.95

Tristar International
New York, NY 10010

**NEW GLADIATOR ARMOR SET**

"For your little soldiers! Includes helmet,

breastplate, shield and sword." Lions and Christians are optional. Also, Roman soldier set with handy axe for chopping off heads available.

$19.95 plus $2.00 postage

F.A.O. Schwarz
P.O. Box 218
Parsippany, NJ 07054

## EAGLE FORCE UZI COMBAT SET

Let your child participate fully in Middle East terrorist games with this lifelike replica of the Israeli Uzi machine pistol. With the hand grenade, 45' automatic, and combat knife, the kids in the neighborhood can practice hijacking airplanes.

$9.95 at Woolworth stores

## SIT AND DRUMS

The toy guaranteed to make both mother and grandmother stark raving mad. This set, designed for three year olds and up, includes:

7-½"  Snare Drum
9"     Bass Drum
5"     Bongo Drum
Cow Bell

Xylophone
2 Drum Sticks

$13.95 at Woolworth stores

# NIGHT CRAWLER

"It really crawls." This large realistic replica of a tarantula moves and glows in the dark. Perfect for putting in Mommy and Daddy's bed at night.

$2.74

REMCO TOYS
New York, NY 10010

# COME PLAY CLEANING SET

Teach your daughter to be a good little housewife early in life, before she gets any left-wing ideas about having a career. Comes with broom, dustpan, and apron.

$2.29 at Woolworth stores

# TWEETY PIE

This doll drinks, moves, and wets all over her diaper. Fortunately, it's fully washable.

$19.99 at Woolworth stores.

# 17

# NOVELTIES

**PET HERPES**

Yes, it's really true. This little rubber creature rops any imaginable list of disgusting presents.

$6.98 including postage

Gifts in Bad Taste
20926 Ventura Blvd., #600
Woodland Hills, CA 91364

**THE SPERM BANK**

This ceramic, item, cast in the shape of human sperm, is six inches long and, according to the makers, "comes with its own certificate of deposit."

# THE SPERM BANK

**SPERM BANK**

## You Can Bank on it!

The Sperm Bank is guaranteed to be a conversation piece wherever it's displayed. The ceramic cast, glazed finish bank is over six inches long and comes with its own certificate of deposit. It's available for $14.95 plus $1.00 handling from:

**SBA Inc., P.O. Box 361,
Roseville, MI 48066**

Visa and MasterCards Accepted.

ALLOW 4 TO 6 WEEKS DELIVERY

Michigan residents add 4% sales tax.

$14.95 plus $1.00 handling

SBA Inc.
P.O. Box 361
Roseville, MD 48066


## FLICK-A-HIGH

Combination pipe/pool stick, pipe/umbrella, or pipe/cane. Unscrew handle for self-lighting pipe with replaceable Bic. Also built-in spoon, stash cap, and joint adapter.

| | |
|---|---|
| Pipe/Pool Stick | $49.95 |
| Pipe/Umbrella | $29.95 |
| Pipe/Cane | $24.95 |
| | Plus $2.50 shipping |

Mackenzie Company
Box 29
Calabasas, CA 91302


## ASS KICKIN' LIGHT SWITCHES

Charming crude plates for light switches, with the switches sticking out of the genital area of the "Mutha" or the "Biker."

$7.95 plus $1.25 postage

Lite Switches
P.O. Box 1025
Agoura, CA 91301

## FASTY-ITY BELT

This charming item is not exactly the gift for someone who is sensitive about his or her weight. The Fast-Ity Belt is a plastic muzzle that keeps food out of a person's mouth the way a chastity belt keeps certain things out of other areas. Lock not included.

$5.95

Contemporary Novelties, Inc.
10758 Trenton
St. Louis, MO 63132

## POT BUST

This flower pot, shaped like a pair of rather large breasts, looks as though it could nurse the plants. A bit distracting, though.

Pleasure Chest Sales Ltd.
20 W. 20th St.
New York, NY 10011

## DUKES OF HAZZARD PAPERWARE

Guaranteed to make you lose whatever you put on the plates or in the cups. Gross plus.

8 7" Plates     $1.10
8 9" Plates     $1.15
8 Cups          $1.10
5 Party Hats    $1.35

Maid of Scandandvia
Minneapolis, MN 55416


## SKULL BEER MUG

This handcrafted bone china beer mug in the shape of a grinning human skull holds 1 quart.

$13.95 including postage

Mackenzi Company
Box 29
Calabasas, CA 91302


## BEVERLY HILLS KITTY LITTER

This ritzy kitty litter consists of shredded greenbacks. If you don't have a cat, you can throw it at weddings.

$10.00 per box postpaid

The Tolman Geffs Company
4300 Campus Drive, #209
Newport Beach, CA 92660

## HOUSE OF HORROR STUDIOS

Great little items to leave around the house, wear out to dinner, or pop out of the closet to surprise your spouse. Does not come with cardio-pulmonary resuscitation unit.

### Masks

| | |
|---|---|
| Pirate | $20.00 |
| Sheik | $20.00 |
| Vampire Skull | $22.00 |
| Deranged | $22.50 |
| Virgil | $22.50 |
| Old Bob | $22.50 |
| Mutant Warrior | $27.00 |
| Vampire | $26.00 |
| Yomad | $26.00 |
| B.E.M. | $26.00 |
| Mutant | $26.00 |
| Mummy | $26.00 |
| Living Death | $26.00 |
| Tentaloid | $26.00 |
| Sandak | $26.00 |
| Ecilan Tuu | $26.00 |
| Wolf Man | $26.00 |

### Hands

| | |
|---|---|
| Monster | $25.00 pair |
| Alien #1 | $25.00 pair |
| Alien #2 | $25.00 pair |
| Fly Claw | $15.00 each |

### Goodies

| | |
|---|---|
| Severed Finger | $ 1.25 |
| The Eye | $ 1.25 |
| Antenna (pair) | $ .50 |
| Li'l Monster #1 | $10.00 |
| Li'l Monster #2 | $10.00 |
| Old Bob | $29.00 |

| | |
|---|---|
| Devil | $26.00 |
| Tule Monster | $35.00 |
| Beast | $40.00 |
| Werewolf | $40.00 |
| Fly | $40.00 |
| B.O.T. | $55.00 |
| Sea Beast | $45.00 |

Add $1.50 per item for postage

House of Horror Studios
713 S. Victory Blvd.
Burbank, CA 91502

## PECKER UPPERS

1. Little Pecker Pencil Tops—Penis shaped erasers 6 for $3.95
2. Pretty Little Thing: Penis-tipped lipstick. $2.50
3. Flick-My-Dick: Penis shaped lighter $4.50
4. Right Prescription Bottle: Open the cap and out pops a penis $2.50

Add $2.65 for postage

Stamford Hygienic
P.O. Box 932
Stamford, CT 06904

## STOP SIGNS

Modeled on the international traffic signs (red circle with a line across), these 10" by 10" signs cover activities you'll never find a stop sign for.

- ★ NO BULLSHITTING
- ★ NO FOOLING AROUND ON COMPANY TIME
- ★ NO HANGING AROUND

## SMOKECASE

"Be Cool, Keep Your Smoke Cool."
"Smokecase is the world's first temperature controlled take-anywhere pocketsize carrying case designed to keep smoking materials cool, fresh, and moist in the period between their removal from the refrigerator or freezer until the time they are actually smoked." If you keep your Marlboros (or, god forbid, marijuana) next to your ice cream, this is the product for you.

$26.95 postpaid

Smokecase
P.O. Box 6279
Spartanburg, S.C. 29304

## LOOK-ALIKE DRIVER'S LICENSE

"THE GENUINE UNI-PHOTO ID actually resembles your state DRIVER LICENSE. Guaranteed results." What results?

$12.00 plus $1.00 postage

Uni-Photo
Box 3787
Edmond, OK
73083

## THE DE LOREAN FAN CLUB

Poor John got caught, but he evidently hasn't lost all his admirers. For $9.95 plus $1.00 postage, you get a T-shirt reading "De Lorean School of High Finance," a "Toot for De Lorean" bumper sticker, and 25 De Lorean jokes.

The De Lorean Fan Club
P.O. Box 610
Walmanalo, Hawaii 96795

## MAGNIFICENT BRASS PAPERWEIGHT

The ad says this deadringer for brass knuckles is "For novelty paperweight use only." Right.

$8.95 plus $.50 shipping

Bruck's
Box 10456
Jacksonville, FL 32207

## PIG SNOUT GLASSES

"For traveling and partying 'inhognito.' "
This lovely item is from "The Pork Avenue
Collection, devoted entirely to the swiner
things in life."

Pig Snout Glasses, 2 pair for $8.00 postpaid
Pork Avenue Collection Catalog, $1.00

Hog Wild
Faneuil Hall Market #443
Boston, MA 02109

## ICEBREAKERS AND SCORECARDS

Imagine you're at a party and a stranger
comes up and hands you a card that reads, "If
you want to see what's under my clothes, just
smile. If not, tear up this card."

Get the idea. A way to "break the ice" and
to really "score" without saying a word. The
only problem is making sure the people you
hand them to can read—no small dilemma for
the audience for such cards as:

"I really like your outfit. If I can talk you out of it, just smile. If not, tear up this card."

"If you'd like me to test the effectiveness of your birth control, just smile! If not, tear up this card."

"If you'd like to view an adult movie, just smile! If not, tear up this card."

"If you'd like to share a shower together, just smile! If not, tear up this card."

"I bet you ten dollars that I'll get you into bed or get you to smile. If you want to bet, just tear up this card."

Cards are $1.00 each, $10.00 for 14, $20.00 for 30 $.95 postage on orders less than $5.00

Icebreakers
P.O. Box 758
Cerritos, CA 90701

## TAKE IT OFF PRODUCTS

Nothing like a bunch of nudes to liven up a cocktail party or meeting. Take the following items:

1. Penthouse Swizzle Strippers ($5.95): "Stir your drink and they strip before

your eyes; get dressed again when they dry off."

2. Centerfold Glasses (4, $9.88): "Add ice and they undress before your eyes. Available are girls, guys, and couples."

3. Pin-up Air Fresheners ($.99): Blondes, brunettes, and redheads.

4. Super Stud Stripper Pens ($2.50): "Tip it over and they strip before your eyes."

5. Nude Ice Cubes ($1.95): "Great for popsicles."

6. Nude Cigarette Lighter ($1.59): Full color nude

Adolf's
2607 Hennepin
Minneapolis, MN 55408


## PENIS MUGS

Mugs with a handle that is actually molded from a cast of your own penis. Just imagine the look on your date's face when you serve her an after dinner drink.

$50

Kospec Studios
RD 2, Box 311K
Route 44    55
Highland, NY 12528

## ACRE OF HELL

"ACRE OF HELL. Recorded in your name. Plus, the Map of Hades, artistically illustrated on framable 18" x 24" parchment."

$14.95 plus $1.00 postage

PFV Enterprises
Box 1261
Clearlake, CA 95422

## RHODESIAN PSYCHOLOGICAL WARFARE LEAFLETS

"Set of 4 depicting terror and death as the way of Communist Terrorists . . . originals airdropped over Rhodesia's Operational Areas . . . Free 'Reward for Reporting Terrorists' with each order."

$9.95 postpaid

SAS Publishers
P.O. Box 2776
Hendersonville, NC 28793

## MARKED CARDS

"Best in the country! Impossible to detect!"

$8.00 per deck, 3 for $21.00

Pennsylvania Success
Box 14190
Philadelphia, PA 19138

## CORDLESS ELECTRIC CARD SHUFFLER

Takes away that time-consuming, strenuous card-party chore. Shuffles up to 2 decks.

$9.95 plus $2.50 postage

Spencer Gifts
J-67 Spencer Bldg.
Atlantic City, NJ 08411

## CLOCK SUCKER

A sucker imprinted with hands and numbers, and the words "Clock Sucker." "Don't call them one. Send them one." $4.98

Conway Enterprises
P.O. Box 2051
Palmer, Alaska 99645

## COCKSUCKER

"Really good candy on a stick, in penis

shape. Sneak one in her desk drawer." $1.00 each, min. purchase 5 (plus $1.00 postage)

Dynamite Sales Co.
P.O. Box 763
Van Nuys, CA 91408

# 18

# PERIODICALS

*HUSTLER* $3.50 Monthly

The quintessential gross magazine. Origina-
tor of the "gynecologist's eye" photographs of
female private parts. Disgusting cartoons (e.g.,
man in a suit holding a glass in his brown
stained hands, saying to a woman, "How'd
you guess I'm a proctologist?"). Monthly "Bits
& Pieces" column shows such lovely stuff as
somebody slicing a penis with a knife, etc. The
articles are relatively mild by comparison.

*FANGORIA* $2.95 Eight times a year

Billed as the magazine of "Monsters, Aliens,
Bizarre Creatures". Opening the front cover of
a recent issue revealed a full-color picture of a
machete slicing into the face of a teenager
(from Friday The 13th, Part 2). Inside is filled

with gory pictures from the bloodiest horror and monster movies. Don't leave this near the dinner table.


## WEEKLY WORLD NEWS

Some headlines from a recent issue:

MERMAID FAMILY FOUND IN PACIFIC
EVIL VOODOO DOCTOR TORTURES HOUSEWIFE
 WITH POISON TOADS
GHOST SHIP SPOTTED IN DEVIL'S TRIANGLE
WORLD'S TINIEST TRANSEXUAL


## SOLDIER OF FORTUNE $3.00 Monthly

"The Journal of Professional Adventurers." Magazine devoted to the glorification of the commando. Detailed articles cover all the current guerrilla wars, plus weapons testing. Can equip a battalion from the advertisements—and you'd better hurry, if the magazine gets its way.


## NATIONAL EXAMINER $.50 Weekly

Some headlines in a recent issue:

PRINCESS GRACE IS ALIVE
BEWARE OF THE VAMPIRE DOCTORS

## *PREVENTION* $1.25 Monthly

Full of articles like "Linoleic Acid—A Fat You Can't Live Without"; "Put Pectin To Work For You"; "The Amazing Benefits of New Fiber Supplements." The sum total of the advice in a year's worth of issues could have you ingesting hundreds of pills a day. Ads feature such goodies as "Enzyme Digestant Tablets," "Dessicated Argentine Beef Liver," and "Bee Pollen." Enough to make you lose your appetite for a month.

## *GLOBE* $.50 Weekly

Some headlines in a recent issue:

HOW JFK KILLED HIMSELF
BLUEBELLS CURE ARTHRITIS
TWIN TAKES OVER AS DI VANISHES
TRUCK WHEELS SQUASHED OUR HEADS LIKE
    MELONS

## *STAR* $.50 Weekly

Some headlines in a recent issue:

WHY WE CAN'T SCREAM IN OUR DREAMS

HOW TV'S SPOILED STARS GET THEIR
   $$$MILLION SALARIES—AND ANYTHING
   ELSE THEY WANT
COWBOY VICAR LEAVES FLOCK TO PUNCH
   CATTLE

## DETECTIVE MAGAZINES Most $1.25 Monthly

The titles of the individual publications are irrelevant, since they all look alike. Article titles in one, FRONT PAGE DETECTIVE, include: "Clue of the Bloody Cane in the Canal"; "Flaming Death of the Brutalized Nude"; "The Sunset Strip Slayer Was A Fantasy Freak"; "He Raped Out of Love For Womanhood." The gorier and more sordid the crime, the better. Great nighttime reading.

## RAW: *The Graphix Magazine of Abstract Depressionism* $5.95

If you don't know what abstract depressionism is, you will after spending $5.95 on this rather bizarre art publication.

## READER'S DIGEST $1.50 Monthly

"The World's Most-Read Magazine." The perfect gift for your grandmother—if she can read articles like "How to Win a Pullet Surprise"; "I'm Afraid of My Own Child"; and "The Little Leaguer I'll Never Forget" without falling out of her rocker. The canned vanilla pudding of publications.

## *NATIONAL ENQUIRER* $.65 Weekly

Some headlines in a recent issue:

SHOCKING STUDY REVEALS: MEN DON'T LIKE WOMEN

SPACE ALIENS ARE BEING BEAMED DOWN TO EARTH

WOMAN HOLES UP IN EX-HUBBY'S GARAGE FOR 17 MONTHS

MR. T. RIPS ARMS OFF HIS SUIT FOR RESTAURANT SCENE

## *EASYRIDER* $2.00 Monthly

"Entertainment for Adult Bikers." No comment.

# 19

# PETS

## TIMBERSHEPERD

Timberwolf/German Shepherd hybrid. "The Ultimate in Family Protection. Protective loyal companion for Home-Apt.-Retreat-Camping-Hiking . . . Special Operations."

LRRP Security Services
Box 507M
Leesville, SC 29070

# 20

# POSTERS

## HORROR AND MONSTER POSTERS

From: The Poster Pit
      RD3 Box 195
      Catawissa, PA 17820

The following movie posters are great for Aunt Edna's room:

| | |
|---|---|
| Blood Bath | $ 7.00 |
| Countess Dracula | $10.00 |
| Eaten Alive | $15.00 |
| Ghost In The Invisible Bikini | $ 7.50 |
| Hands of the Ripper | $ 4.00 |
| House of the 7 Corpses | $ 8.00 |
| Orgy of the Living Dead | $ 4.50 |
| Slumber Party Massacre | $ 8.50 |
| The Thirsty Dead | $ 4.00 |
| Gator Bait | $ 5.00 |
| The Blood Rose | $10.00 |

Scream Blacula Scream .......... $ 7.50
Squirm ......................... $ 6.00
Bloody Mama ................... $ 8.00
Terror Train ................... $ 8.25
The Hot Box ................... $ 7.50

## BIKER POSTERS

Art from Dave Mann. Titles include:

Ride Hard Die Fast
Prison Release
Apehanger Days
Comin' At Ya
Sunset Blvd.
Hollyweed

$5.00 Each

Easyrider Posters
P.O. Box 1025
Agoura, CA 91301

# 21

# RECORDS AND TAPES

DAVID ALLAN COE

This chap has two albums that are "NOT FOR SALE IN STORES." The ad also says "Party records, not for air play."

1. UNDERGROUND ($15.00). Songs like:

    *Little Susie Shallow Throat*
    *Pick 'Em, Lick 'Em, Stick 'Em*
    *I'd Just like to (not printable) You One*
        *More Time*

2. NOTHING SACRED ($12.00): Songs like:

    *Biggest Lies In The World*
    *I Was Into Whips & Things, and She*
        *Was Into Pain*
    *I Made Linda Lovelace Gag*

Coe Album
Box 1025
Agoura, CA 91301

## GET IN THE MOOD

The ad says these two records will "fill anybody's imagination with steamy sexual experiences."

1. SEX LOVE STORY: "An erotic tale of the most stimulating kind."
2. SENSUOUS MEN AND WOMEN TOGETHER: "Live sex concert recorded in intimate detail."

Records or cassettes $6.95 each, both for $11.95

Stamford Hygenic
P.O. Box 932
Stamford, CT 06904

## MUSIC TO MAIM BY

Nothing like having a date over and putting the score from a movie like DAWN OF THE DEAD, MANIAC, or THE BLACK BELLY OF THE TARANTULA. Dance to the sound track from IT'S ALIVE 2, SWAMP THING, INSEMINOID, CREEPSHOW, MAD MAX,

PIRANHA, THE HOWLING, or HALLO-
WEEN II. Neck to ANDY WARHOL'S
FRANKENSTEIN, NIGHT OF THE LIVING
DEAD, or MARTIN. Yuch.

$7.98 each plus $1.12 postage

Fangoria Record Shelf
475 Park Avenue South, 8th Fl.
New York, NY 10016

## YOU CAN HEAR VIET NAM

"1-hour cassette recording of helicopter
gunship radio-traffic during VC/NVA attack
on Long Binh/Bien Hoa area, February 26,
1969. With 40 page transcript book."

$15 postpaid

Bien Hoa Productions
Box 56
Fayetteville, AR 72702

## PAULA LANE MUSIC TO MAKE LOVE BY

Looking like Marilyn Monroe has kept Paula
Lane busy on TV and in clubs. Now you can
buy a collection of romantic songs in the voice
of the dead sex symbol.

$7.95 plus $1.50 postage

Paula Lane
P.O. Box 8051
Van Nuys, CA 91409

## AUDIO SUBLIMINAL SUGGESTION (A.S.S.)

"When you use an A.S.S. recording, you will have the latest technology working for you, designed to make women submit to you and to their own hidden desires. You can stimulate their subconscious fantasies, making them want to react sexually."

30 min. cassette $14.95

Dugent Publishing Corp.
2355 Salzedo St., Suite 204
Coral Gables, FL 33134

## SEX SOUNDS

SENSATIONAL SOUNDS OF SUPER SEX. "puts you in the mood with all the sighs, slurps, moans, groans, grunts and squishes of Hot and Bothered Teenagers." Record or cassette. $7.95

21st Century Products
P.O. Box 1048
Scarsdale, NY 10583

# 22

# SERVICES

## PHOTO DEVELOPMENT

"Personal and Private. Personal Photo will process any 5247 or 5293 film you send in STRICT PRIVACY. These are the films used by movie pros to make stars look their best in those special scenes."

$6.95 for 2 rolls of either 5247 (ASA 100) or 5293 (ASA 250)

Personal Photo
15182 Bolsa Chica Road, Suite B
Huntington Beach, CA 92647

## DIVORCES

1. "One Day Divorce. Dominican-Haitian-Mexican. $325.00 and up."

P.O. Box 169
Peekskill, NY 10566

2. "Divorce $212 terms, By Mail."

Action
Box 712
Dahlonega, GA 30533

## HERPES DATING SERVICE

For $55 Clement Mosseri says that he will mail you three to ten names of fellow herpes sufferers within 45 days. Name of the firm won't even appear on return address.

HERPES DATING SERVICE
Manhattan Beach, California

## EASY CREDIT

"No Credit? Bad Credit? No Problem. Receive Mastercard/Visa/Major Credit Card. Free Brochure, Send Self-Addressed Stamped Envelope." Hmmm.

Consumer Credit Council
P.O. Box 1163
Sunnymead, CA 92388

# 23

# SEX AIDS

LOVE COSMETICS

From: Stamford Hygienic
      P.O. Box 932
      Stamford, CT 06904

1. Lovers Lubricant: "Deliciously flavored, fragrant, slippery, wet and wild." In Strawberry Fruit. $5.95

2. Erection Lotion: "A mint flavored roll-on that gets it up when you get it on." $8.95

3. Mr. Hard On: "Rise up and conquer with this delicious cinnamon flavored roll-on cream. Active ingredients stimulate the penis to make getting hard easy." $5.95

4. Nipple Nectar: "Let him taste the sweet, full fruit of your ripe breasts." Comes in Coconut, Strawberry, Chocolate, and Banana. $4.50

5. Hap-Penis: "Easy come—easy grow." $6.95

6. Hot Stuff: "Gets hot when you breathe on it." Strawberry and cinnamon. $7.95

7. Sta-Hard: "A desensitizing lubricant to prevent premature ejaculation." $6.95

8. Orgy Butter: "This famous, sensual, strawberry-flavored lubricant makes it easy to slip into tight places." $5.95

9. Female Bliss Cream: "This special stimulating cream for women will envelop her in a warm glow of pleasurable anticipation and make it hard for her to say no." $5.95

10. Lovers Sampler: "Explore with Lemon-Lime Penis Lube, Kumquat flavored Female Power, delicious Honeydew Orgy Love Oil, and Rasberry Emotion Lotion." $5.95

FROM: Pleasure Products
P.O. Box 5973-198
Sherman Oaks, CA 91413

1. Body Gell-O: "Strawberry flavored. Fragrant. Slippery. Washable. Non-Staining." $6.00

2. Peter Licker (Cherry or Banana) and Pussy Licker (Strawberry or Tropical Fruit): "Here's the new way to enjoy oral sex." $5.00

3. Nipple Lick'ems: Coconut, Strawberry, Chocolate, Cherry, and Pina Colada. $5.00

FROM: Valentine Products, Inc.
P.O. Box 6400
Newtown, CT 06470

1. Swedish Erotica Lover's Lube: "Makes love taste sweeter than ever before." Strawberry, Lemon, or Grape. $5.95

2. Mr. Prolong: "Just one blast from this special topical spray and the sensitive corona of your erect penis is lightly numbed." $8.95

3. Anal Lube: "Things go more smoothly when you use this specially flavored lube in cinnamon." $5.95

# 24

# T-SHIRTS

MIRA SHIRTS

* THE SPLATTER SHIRT ("Bloodier than ever" Blood red on white) $6.50
* INSECTIVOROUS ("Four color masterpiece. Behold it's multi-colored body and blood-red fangs") $11.00

Mira
2520 N. Lincoln Ave.
Box 252
Chicago, IL 60614

L.E.W.D. (LIMITED EDITION WEAPONS DESIGNS) T-SHIRTS

* SCATTER 'EM WITH A SHOTGUN
* GUN CONTROL IS BEING ABLE TO HIT YOUR TARGET

* PEACE THROUGH SUPERIOR FIRE-
  POWER

T-Shirts $8.50 postpaid

Cloudland Enterprises
P.O. Box 3611
Chattanooga, TN 37404

## BIKER 'ONE LINERS'

Choose your favorite, available in T-shirt, cap, or underwear:

* IF LITTLE GIRLS ARE MADE OF SUGAR AND SPICE, WHY DO THEY TASTE LIKE TUNA
* BIKERS ARE SO HORNY, EVEN THE CRACK OF DAWN ISN'T SAFE
* WHAT MOST CALL PUSSY, I CALL LUNCH
* A WOMAN'S PLACE IS ON MY FACE
* LIQUOR UP FRONT, POKER IN THE REAR
* I'M HIS 'CAUSE HE GIVES GOOD FACE
* SHOW ME YOUR TITS
* SHOW ME YOUR DICK
* WHITE, AND PROUD OF IT
* RIDE HARD—DIE FREE

T-Shirts $6.50 plus $1.25 for design

Adolf's
2607 Hennepin Avenue South
Minneapolis, MN 55408


## PHOENIX T-SHIRTS

* BE A MAN AMONG MEN—JOIN THE RHODESIAN ARMY
* PATIENCE MY ASS! I'M GOING OUT AND KILL SOMETHING!
* NUKE IRAN
* MERCENARIES DO IT FOR PROFIT
* SPECIAL FORCES—LIVING BY CHANCE, LOVING BY CHOICE, KILLING BY PROFESSION
* SUPPORT AFGHAN FREEDOM FIGHTERS
* SOUTHEAST ASIA WAR GAMES — 2ND PLACE

T-Shirts $7.95 plus $1.25 postage

Phoenix Associates
Box 687
Boulder, CO 80306


## OLIVE-DRAB T-SHIRTS

* BETTER DEAD THAN RED

* KILL A COMMIE FOR MOMMY
* I'D RATHER BE KILLING COM-
MUNISTS

T-shirts $8.00 postpaid

RJS Shirts
6 Karen Court
Scotch Plains, NJ 07076

## DIRTY SHIRTS

* HAPPINESS COMES IN SNATCHES
* SIT ON A HAPPY FACE
* GENUINE MUSTACHE RIDES 5
CENTS
* YOU CAN'T BEAT MY MEAT
* SCREW IMPORTS, BUY AMERICAN
* AN ELEVEN IS A 10 THAT
SWALLOWS
* I'M IN HEAT
* MY BODY IS AN OUTLAW. IT'S
WANTED ALL OVER TOWN
* SCREW HOUSEWORK
* LOOKIN' FOR 10 POUNDS OF
SWINGING MEAT
* YOU TOUCH MY TITS I'LL BUST
YOUR BALLS
* DON'T ASK ME I'M JUST A DUMB
CUNT
* BEND OVER, I'LL DRIVE
* GO SUCK A FART

* NO TEENIE WEENIES
* MY FACE IS LEAVING AT TEN—BE ON IT
* TOO DRUNK TO FUCK

T-shirts $8.00 plus $1.00 shipping

Biker's Candy Store
P.O. Box 3069
Thousand Oaks, CA 91360

## BLACK T-SHIRTS

* IF YOU CAN'T FIX IT, FUCK IT
* AS LONG AS I HAVE A FACE, YOU'LL HAVE A PLACE TO SIT
* MESS WITH THE BEST, DIE LIKE THE REST
* I SNATCH KISSES AND VICE VERSA
* IF GOD HADN'T MEANT MAN TO EAT PUSSY, HE WOULDN'T HAVE SHAPED IT LIKE A TACO
* MY PHILOSOPHY IS QUITE SIMPLE, IF YA CAN'T EAT IT OR SCREW IT . . . PISS ON IT!

T-shirts $8.00 plus $.50 postage

Black halter tops, tank tops, or French cuts

* BEAT ME BITE ME
  WHIP ME FUCK ME

LIKE THE DIRTY PIG
THAT I AM CUM ALL
OVER MY TITS AND
TELL ME THAT YOU
LOVE ME THEN GET
THE FUCK OUT!

$7.50 halter tops/$8.50 tank tops/$9.50
French cut

Coco
P.O. Box 451
Calabasas, CA 91302

## THE SHOOTISTS

* THE IRS DOES IT TO EVERYONE
* FISHERMEN DO IT WITH BIGGER
  RODS
* FIREMEN DO IT WITH A BIGGER
  HOSE
* GOLFERS DO IT WITH CLEANER
  BALLS
* HUNTERS DO IT IN THE BUSH

T-shirts $12.95 plus $1.50 postage

The Shootists
7655 E. Redfield, Suite 8
Scottsdale, AZ 85260

## IF SHE'S GOT 'EM, FLAUNT 'EM

* BET YOU CAN'T EAT JUST ONE
* TASTY CAKES
* BOOBS
* FULL BLOOM
* MY BODY BELONGS TO ME, BUT I SHARE

T-shirts $7.95 plus $.95 postage

Dugent Corp.
2355 Salzedo Street
Coral Gables, FL 33134

## FUCK WHAT PEOPLE THINK T-SHIRTS

Shirt has a couple dozen phrases, including:

FUCK THE PHONE COMPANY; FUCK OFF; FUCK PAY TOILETS; FUCK THERAPY; FUCK SMOG; FUCK VIRGINITY.

T-shirt $7.95

Rockart
109A Palm Street
Nashua, NH 03060

# GUCCIONE GRAPHICS

* IN OUTER SPACE, NOBODY CAN HEAR YOU FART
* DON'T ARGUE WITH YOUR WIFE, JUST DICKER!
* HEY LITTLE GIRL, WANNA PIECE OF CANDY?
* I'M NOT WEARING ANY UNDERWEAR. FILM AT 11.
* MINE'S BIGGER
* I DO, BUT NOT WITH YOU
* I THOUGHT YOU WERE DEAD
* SOUNDS LIKE BULLSHIT TO ME
* LISTEN TO WHAT I MEAN, NOT WHAT I SAY
* SAVE A MOUSE. EAT A PUSSY.
* LET ME LICK YOUR THIGHS
* EAT A BOX LUNCH AT THE "Y"
* IT'S BETTER TO BE PISSED OFF THAN PISSED ON

T-shirts $6.99 plus $2.00 shipping

Guccione Graphics
1080 S. Cypress St., Bldg. F
La Habra, CA 90631

# S.I.N.

*         S.I.N.              (FRONT)
    SEX IS NORMAL

## FELLATIO, MASTURBATION, CUNNILINGUS, etc. (BACK)

T-shirt $8.95

S.I.N. Sex Is Normal
P.O. Box 02884
Detroit, MI 48202

## MUTANT OF OMAHA

T-shirt reads: Mutant of Omaha: Nuclear Holocaust Insurance.

$7.95 postpaid

Mutant of Omaha
Box 2432
Omaha, NB 68108

## MUTANTS FOR NUCLEAR ENERGY

Fun message comes on beige, sky blue, heather grey, navy, or burgundy shirt. $9.00 postpaid

Merry Mutant Products
Fontana Center
Suite 1077
Tulsa, OK 74145

## MARILYN MONROE

Bet hardly anyone on your block has a T-shirt with a reproduction of Marilyn Monroe's original USO Entertainer ID Card.

$10.00 from Class Act
          41 W. 36th St.
          New York, NY 10018

## MORE LITERATE T-SHIRTS

It may not mark you as a literary snob, but what do you think about someone who walks around with a picture of Shopenhauer or Dostoevsky on his or her chest? Others available include:

| | |
|---|---|
| T.S. Eliot | Sartre |
| Trollope | Machiavelli |
| Charlotte Bronte | Nietzche |
| Samuel Johnson | Camus |
| Adam Smith | Wittgenstein |
| Gandhi | Plato |
| Kafka | Bach |
| Freud | Proust |
| Darwin | Dante |

    $10.00 plus $1.00 shipping

Historical Products
Box 220KC
Cambridge, MA 02238

# 25

# TATTOOING

## 50 PIECE PROFESSIONAL TATTOO OUTFIT

- — Sheets of Designs
- — Power Box (Heavy Duty)
- — Tattoo Machines (Outliner and Shader)
- — Foot Switch
- — Line Cord
- — Bottles of Assorted Colors
- — Bottle of Stencil Powder
- — Sheet of Plastic Stencil Material
- — Stencil Cutter
- — Extra Outliner Needles
- — Extra Shader Needles
- — Color Tray for Tattoo Pigments

$495.00 plus $10.00 postage

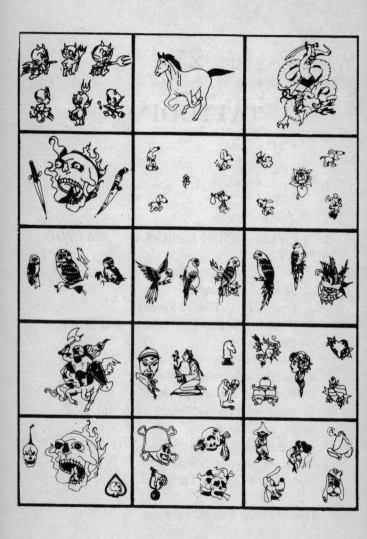

S & W Tattooing, Inc.
P.O. Box 263
East Northport, NY 11731

## TATTOO DESIGNS
$1.00 each. With stencils $8.00

## TATTOO REMOVAL

"TATTOOED? EMBARRASSED? GET RID OF 'EM!"

"Several European chemists developed a lotion which will remove almost any tattoo, providing, you adhere to the simple step by step instructions which come with each Do-It-Yourself kit."

Entire kit costs $30.00

Tatex International Co., Ltd.
P.O. Box 494
Pickering, Ontario
Canada L1V2R7

# 26

# TELEPHONE NUMBERS

PHONE SEX

Free, recorded love messages—if this is your bag.

| | |
|---|---|
| LIVE WIRE | 1-212-976-2626 |
| HIGH SOCIETY | 1-212-976-2727 |
| SEX CONNECTION | 1-212-976-2828 |
| HUSTLER CENTERFOLD | 1-212-976-7474 |

DIAL-A-SOAP

If you can believe it, America's first telephone soap opera. This service allows you a 60 second listen in to a simulated party call between the folks at "America Magazine" and their friends and lovers. If you get hooked and you live in Alaska, it's an expensive hobby.

1-212-976-6363

# 27

# TOYS FOR ADULTS

## TV BAND RADIO

"Don't miss a soap opera when you're at the beach." As if television wasn't bad enough to watch, here's a portable radio that allows you to pick up the sound. $29.90 Magnavox #1305

## DIGITAL SCALE

"Digital scale shows weight at eye level. No more bending or squinting." You step on this scale and hold a portable control in your hand that allows you to read your weight without moving a muscle. Provided, of course, you're not too lazy to weigh yourself in the first place. $59.00 NSC

## EAGLE SCOREMASTER

Adding up pars and bogies becoming too much of a strain? The Eagle Scoremaster is a "fully electronic, digital, computerized scorekeeper." And for those who like to amend the results, "includes an easy-edit feature so you can make corrections for any hole at any time during or after the game." A real bargain at $99.00

## SPEED LISTENING

"The VSC Sound Pacer lets you take advantage of the wealth of knowledge available on spoken word cassettes—in half the normal listening time. It electronically skips over blank spaces between words and syllables." $199

## INSTANT BREATH TEST

Blow into the device to check your alcohol intake. Your wife or husband will love holding this up to your face when you get home from the office Christmas party. $78.00

## THE PHONE THAT QUACKS

Telephone in the shape of a duck decoy.

Simply lift the fowl's head, and you're on the line! $249

## IS STRESS GOING TO YOUR HEAD

"Antache Biofeedback Headset lets you literally listen to tension in your head, neck and shoulder levels." Sounds like a lot of fun. $129.00

## COMPACT SHREDDER

End worries from those legions of people poring through your garbage. This compact paper shredder sits on top of your wastebasket. Insert paper and it automatically turns itself on. $149

## ALL ABOVE ITEMS AVAILABLE FROM:

THE SHARPER IMAGE
P.O. Box 26823
San Francisco, CA 94111
800-344-4444

## RADIATION METER

Prepare for nuclear power plant disasters and atomic war. "With a NWS RAD III you'll know:

1. Which parts of a shelter give the best protection
2. When it's safe to leave.
3. How long you can stay outside
4. When it's safe to return."

$149.95

Oregon Radiation Sciences
7777 Leesburg Pike
Falls Church, VA 22043

## ELECTRONIC SURVEILLANCE SECURITY EQUIPMENT

1. Big Brother Telescreen—"See and hear through walls, ceilings and floors." $395
2. Wireless FM Transmitters—
   300' range $40
   1000' range $75
   2 mi. range $225
3. Shotgun Microphone $195.
4. KODAK Surveillance Camera $395
5. Camera in Butane Lighter $165
6. Telephone voice scramblers $295
7. Infrared Night Vision Scope $295
8. Letterbomb Visualizer Spray $ 35

Professional's Catalog $20
General Catalog $2

Surveillance Device Schematics Portfolio $20

**MICROTRON**
500 Hawley Bldg.
Wheeling, WV 26003

# 28

# VACATIONS

## HEAD TOURS

This travel agency specializes in junkets to Asia, where the male tourist can sample the exotic delights of Oriental women. Not recommended for second honeymoons.

Head Tours
1742 2nd Ave. #207
New York, NY 10028

## BARE VISTAS

Want to take a vacation but don't know what to wear? Solve the problem with a visit to a nudist colony. Bring tanning oil and a wide smile.

Sources of information:

1. Nudist Newsletter       $3.00
   Fun Club
   Box 428
   Bellflower, CA 90706

2. 32 page booklet       $3.00
   Sun West
   P.O. Box 85204
   Los Angeles, CA 90072

## SURVIVAL

"The purpose of our class is to teach you to defend and protect yourself and your family against natural disasters, anarchy, nuclear attack, or economic collapse."

Cost of 2 day course     $195.00

Survival Worldwide
P.O. Box 7304
Reno, Nevada 89502

## SOLDIER OF FORTUNE

Soldier of Fortune Military Arms and Collector's Show. Don't miss the chance to vacation with other adventurers and learn how you can arm yourself for the next insurrection.

For information, write:

SOLDIER OF FORTUNE
P.O. Box 693
Boulder, CO 80306

# 29

# VIDEO GAMES

**HALLOWEEN (Wizard Video)**

In this sickie—billed as "The Game Where HE Comes Home"—the player takes the role of Laurie, the victimized babysitter in the horror movie HALLOWEEN, and tries to save the children from the homicidal maniac. Great fun.

**THE TEXAS CHAINSAW MASSACRE (Wizard Video)**

Here the player becomes that loveable slaughterhouse maniac, Leatherface, who attempts to kill all the game's possible victims with his chainsaw. Wonderful hand-eye training, if mass murder is your hobby.

# HALLOWEEN

## VIDEO GAME CARTRIDGE

# HALLOWEEN

The Game Where *HE* Comes Home!

## CUSTER'S REVENGE (American Multiple Industries)

The General (naked except for hat and boots) dodges dangerous cacti and flying arrows to get to the Indian Maiden (who is tied to a post) to even up the score—so to speak.

## BEAT 'EM AND EAT 'EM (American Multiple Industries)

An oversexed soda jerk is on the loose on a rooftop, shooting his precious bodily fluids into the gaping mouths of streetwalkers below. Every time the ladies swallow, you score a point.

## X-HOT STUFF (Computer Kinetics Corporation)

This is a maze-game similar to Pac-Man. The "enemy" consists of breasts that you, the mouth, must gobble. The goal is to end up in the bed in the middle of the screen for treats that range from deep-throat gratification to back-door loving, Greek style.

## PORNOPOLY

Like monopoly, only with properties like

Satisfaction Avenue and Kinky Place. The goal is to retain money and at least one article of clothing.

## STREETLIFE

You're a pimp who's trying to make a living in this game for the Apple II computer. You must decide such things as which streetcorners will yield the best profit, which cops and thugs to avoid, and how to deal with occupational hazards like VD.

# 30

# WEAPONS

## BLOW GUN

"SILENT, POWERFUL, ACCURATE, HITS LIKE RIFLE BULLET." This "ideal gift" has a 200 foot range, shoots a dart at 300 ft/sec, and is guaranteed for 15 years. A must for your next trip to the Amazon.

Compact 4-1/2' model

$9.97 plus $1.95 postage

100 extra darts     $3.50

House of Weapons
Box 794-S
Provo, Utah 84601

## CROSSBOWS

"A medieval art captured in modern form."

Great for castle storming, dragon slaying, and God knows what other sports and hobbies.

| | |
|---|---|
| WCX Wildcat Crossbow | $189.00 |
| Barnett Imp Pistol Crossbow | $ 49.95 |

Timberwolf Cutlery
P.O. Box 757
Clanton, Alabama 35045

## TANKS—$182.00

Nothing like a tank for rush hour traffic—perfect for parking on big city streets. According to ads, $262,000 tanks have sold for as little as $182.00 as surplus. Other bargains for your private army are reportedly M-16 rifles for $4.80, Colt 45s for $1.60, armored cars for $86.50, and grenades for $.46—cheaper than firecrackers, and twice the fun.

For book MILITARY SURPLUS, telling you how to find such bargains, send $12.95 plus sales tax and $1.55 postage to:

Surplus Sales
Box 15544
Austin, TX 78761

# LASER GUNS AND OTHER "BUCK ROGERS" WEAPONS

Handy around the workbench? Try these do-it-yourself projects.

1. BLASTER/DEVASTATOR DEVICE: "Produces electrical plasma discharges capable of burning living tissue, stunning or disabling a vicious animal or other attacking objects."
    Plans    $10.00      Kit    $59.50

2. BLACK BOX BLITZER DEVICE: "Protects objects, vehicles, and sensitive areas from instrusion, theft and assault. Protects by producing a painful electric shock field . . ."
    Plans    $10.00      Kit    $59.50

3. PHASOR SHOCK WAVE PISTOL: "All new, high powered, acoustical shock wave pistol produces an intense field of highly directional adjustable frequency shock waves . . . CAUTION, CAUTION, unit produces pain, headache, nausea and extreme irritability in most people as well as animals. Use with discretion."
    Plans    $7.00      Kit    $44.50

4. ION RAY GUN: "Produces directional energetic ions capable of charging up objects, people and inducing shocks without contact."
    Plans    $10.00      Kit    $79.50

5. PARALYZER GUN: "This hand-held

device is only 9" long and weighs a mere 1.5 lbs., yet contains a built-in aiming flashlight and has a two-shot capability. Range is up to 15 feet with an immobilizing effect greater than a handgun owing to the fact of its controlling effect on non-vital organs."

Information Pack      $10.00


Information Unlimited
P.O. Box 716
Amherst, NH 03031


# KNIVES

1. Wilkinson Sword Commando Knife: "The most famous Military issued FIGHTING/SURVIVAL knife ever created."
   $169.00 plus $4.25 shipping
2. Benchmark Ninja: 4" full wedge ground blade. Comes with custom leather sheath and nylon shoulder harness."
   $49.95 plus $3.25 shipping.
3. Kershaw Amphibian Boot Knife: 3-3/4" double wedge ground blade. Comes with leather bootclip scabbard.
   $36.95 plus $2.95 shipping
4. Ka-Bar U.S.M.C. Fighting Knife: 7" blade. "1/32" deep blood grooves lighten and strengthen blade."
   $37.00 plus $4.95 shipping
5. Valor Push Dagger: Comes with leather

wallet carrying case. ". . . makes an ideal self defense/concealment weapon for women."

$19.99 plus $1.25 shipping

6. Combat Thrower Battle Blade. ". . . unsurpassed for its ability to withstand the stress and abuse of throwing."

$35.95 plus $3.95 shipping

7. Black Forest Sword Cane: Concealed blade is 23-1/2" long. Simple twist handle 1/4 turn to release internal catch.

$179.95 plus $8.95 shipping

Select Line Sales
P.O. Box 391
Pearl City, Hawaii 96782


# EXOTIC WEAPONS

Know where to find a FOLDING THROWING STAR? Tired of haunting Woolworths for a WOLF-TEETH CLUB? Got the urge to get your hands on a TELESCOPING NIGHTSTICK or a DEFENDO RING? Everything you want to know about where to get these and other deadly little devices is in a book called *EXOTIC WEAPONS: AN ACCESS BOOK*. Chapter headings include:

Air Guns
Arrow Slings
Bolas

Boomerangs
Capture Nets
Exploding and Armor Piercing Ammo
Flame Guns
Garrotes
Knucks, Saps and Other Impact Weapons
Light Weapons
Machine Guns
Medieval, Ancient and Old Time Weapons
Oriental Weapons
Primitive and Stone Age Weapons
Repulse
Robots
Shockers
Silencers
Slingshots
Smoke Bombs
Switchblades
Talon
Tasers
Tomahawks
Tranquilizer Guns
Underwater Weapons
Whips

Loompanics Unlimited
P.O. Box 1197
Port Townsend, WA 98368

PHASER

"Stop muggers and rapists . . . from 15 feet

away in 2 seconds."

$19.95 plus $2.50 postage

Compass Marketing
535 Fifth Avenue
New York, NY 10017

# 31

# FOR THE TRULY GROSS SHOPPER

## EXPLOSIVES IN THE KITCHEN

| | |
|---|---|
| Instructions for making Napalm | $ 8.95 |
| Instructions for Sugar Explosive | $ 8.95 |
| Instructions for "easy to make, extremely destructive, steel-burning Thermite incendiary" | $12.00 |

All three $20.00

American Industries
P.O. Box 10073
Springfield, MO 65808

MILK MAGAZINES

"Lactating ladies feeding milk to each other and their men."

| | |
|---|---|
| Milk #4 | $7.50 |
| Popping Mamas #1 | $6.00 |
| Popping Mamas #2 | $6.00 |

Marlowe Sales
P.O. Box 9506
No. Hollywood, CA 91609


ENTER THE SIDESHOW

This book is described as the "historical picture album of the most amazing sideshow personalities of all time." Features include:

William Durks, the man with 3 eyes
The incredible "Human Pin Cushion"
Jo-Jo, the "Dog-faced Boy"
Frank Lentini, the three-legged man
The two-headed boy
Grace, the "mule-faced woman"
Eko and Iko, the "Sheep-headed People"
Julia, "The Ugliest Women to Ever Live"

$9.95 plus $1.50 postage

Mason Publishing
P.O. Box 523
Bala Cynwyd, PA 19004

## FOR DRINKERS

"Worried about DWI [Driving While Intoxicated] Convictions? . . . Lower your Breathalyzer Test Results 15% to 18% . . . Save money on . . . Summons—Jail—Your License—Insurance Costs—Personal Injuries—Embarrassing Publicity."

Information Packet $5.00

Information Services, Inc.
7 West Street, Suite 213
Danbury, CT 06810

## REPULSE

This is a weapon that you can use on yourself rather than on your assailant. You pour this vial of stuff that smells exactly like skunk all over yourself. Hopefully, your attacker will be so disgusted he'll flee. Then you can pour the neutralizer on yourself and go your merry way. Ugh.

Defense Corporation
201 W. Cactus Lane
Phoenix, AZ 85027

## IDENTITY CHANGE

"Become someone else: new identity will hide your past. Forget debts, child support and other problems. Free details."

Nu-Way Publishing
Box 919
Ypsilanti, MI 48197

# ZEBRA HAS IT ALL!

**PAY THE PRICE**                                   **(1234, $3.95)**
by Igor Cassini
Christina was every woman's envy and every man's dream. And she was compulsively driven to making it—to the top of the modeling world and to the most powerful peaks of success, where an empire was hers for the taking, if she was willing to PAY THE PRICE.

**PLEASURE DOME**                              **(1134, $3.75)**
by Judith Liederman
Though she posed as the perfect society wife, Laina Eastman was harboring a clandestine love. And within an empire of boundless opulence, throughout the decades following World War II, Laina's love would meet the challenges of fate . . .

**DEBORAH'S LEGACY**                           **(1153, $3.75)**
by Stephen Marlowe
Deborah was young and innocent. Benton was worldly and experienced. And while the world rumbled with the thunder of battle, together they rose on a whirlwind of passion—daring fate, fear and fury to keep them apart!

**FOUR SISTERS**                                      **(1048, $3.75)**
by James Fritzhand
From the ghettos of Moscow to the glamor and glitter of the Winter Palace, four elegant beauties are torn between love and sorrow, danger and desire—but will forever be bound together as FOUR SISTERS.

**BYGONES**                                             **(1030, $3.75)**
by Frank Wilkinson
Once the extraordinary Gwyneth set eyes on the handsome aristocrat Benjamin Whisten, she was determined to foster the illicit love affair that would shape three generations—and win a remarkable woman an unforgettable dynasty!

*Available wherever paperbacks are sold, or order direct from the Publisher. Send cover price plus 50¢ per copy for mailing and handling to Zebra Books, 475 Park Avenue South, New York, N.Y. 10016. DO NOT SEND CASH.*